COUNTRIES OF
THE MIDDLE EAST

By Cory Gunderson

VISIT US AT
WWW.ABDOPUB.COM

Published by ABDO & Daughters, an imprint of ABDO Publishing Company, 4940 Viking Drive, Suite 622, Edina, Minnesota 55435. Copyright ©2004 by Abdo Consulting Group, Inc. International copyrights reserved in all countries. No part of this book may be reproduced in any form without written permission from the publisher.

Printed in the United States.

Edited by: Sheila Rivera
Contributing Editors: Paul Joseph, Chris Schafer, Chad Morse
Graphic Design: Arturo Leyva, David Bullen
Cover Design: Castaneda Dunham, Inc.
Photos: Corbis

Library of Congress Cataloging-in-Publication Data

Gunderson, Cory Gideon.
    Countries of the Middle East / Cory Gunderson.
     p. cm. -- (World in conflict--the Middle East)
    Includes index.
    Summary: Introduces some of the countries of the Middle East, including Syria, Iraq, Iran, Israel, Saudi Arabia, and Egypt, and their role in the on-going tensions that exist in this region.
     ISBN 1-59197-419-4
      1. Middle East--Juvenile literature. [1. Middle East.] I. Title. II. World in conflict (Edina, Minn.). Middle East.

    DS44.G86 2003
    956--dc21

                                                                    200304374

TABLE OF CONTENTS

Overview of the Middle East 4

Egypt 8

Iran 13

Iraq 18

Israel 23

Saudi Arabia 28

Syria 33

Web Sites 39

Timeline 40

Fast Facts 42

Glossary 44

Index 48

OVERVIEW OF THE MIDDLE EAST

The land of the Middle East connects the continents of Africa, Asia, and Europe. This region was the birthplace of Christianity, Islam, and Judaism. What happens in this area often impacts other parts of the world.

Not everyone agrees as to what countries can be labeled "Middle Eastern." Even the region has different names, such as West Asia and the Persian Gulf. Countries often referred to as Middle Eastern are: Bahrain, Cyprus, Iran, Iraq, Israel, Jordan, Kuwait, Lebanon, Oman, Qatar, Saudi Arabia, Syria, the United Arab Emirates, and Yemen.

Some other countries typically labeled as Middle Eastern are: Afghanistan, Kazakhstan, Kyrgyzstan, Pakistan, Tajikistan, Turkmenistan, and Uzbekistan. The African countries of Algeria, Egypt, Libya, Morocco, Sudan, and Tunisia are also considered part of this region. The European country of Turkey is sometimes referred to as Middle Eastern, too.

Countries around the world increasingly communicate and trade with each other. Many Western countries depend on the oil that is produced in many Middle Eastern countries. The United

States is one of these Western countries. In turn, many Middle Eastern countries depend on financial support from some Western nations. Nations across the globe depend on each other to survive and thrive. This means that countries are connected more tightly to each other today than ever before.

Political, religious, and economic strife has created turmoil in the Middle East. This has been especially true in recent centuries. Middle Eastern nations have fought each other for control of oil supplies. Control of land has changed hands often after fighting, too. These neighbors have also fought over religion.

Anger toward Western nations, including the U.S., spread across Arab countries in the late 1940s and the 1950s. Many Western nations supported the 1948 creation of a Jewish nation called Israel. Many Arab nations hated the idea of giving up any land to non-Muslims. This decades-long struggle is known as the Israeli-Palestinian conflict. It is at the center of Arabs' resentment of the U.S. and other Western nations.

Arabs' resentment has not been contained within the region. It impacts countries outside the region and across the globe. The September 11, 2001, terrorist attacks against the U.S. showed this. Osama bin Laden, a Middle Easterner who directed the terrorists' attacks, was angry with the U.S. He resented the U.S. government's interference in Middle East affairs. The attacks were meant to punish the U.S.

The Middle Eastern countries covered in this book are those in the heart of the region. They are also those in the heart of the conflict.

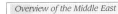

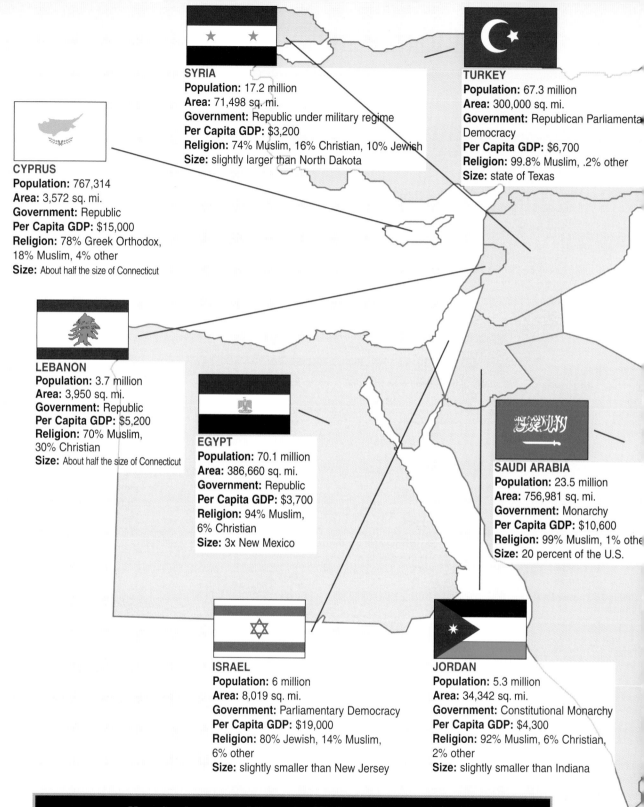

SYRIA
Population: 17.2 million
Area: 71,498 sq. mi.
Government: Republic under military regime
Per Capita GDP: $3,200
Religion: 74% Muslim, 16% Christian, 10% Jewish
Size: slightly larger than North Dakota

TURKEY
Population: 67.3 million
Area: 300,000 sq. mi.
Government: Republican Parliamenta
Democracy
Per Capita GDP: $6,700
Religion: 99.8% Muslim, .2% other
Size: state of Texas

CYPRUS
Population: 767,314
Area: 3,572 sq. mi.
Government: Republic
Per Capita GDP: $15,000
Religion: 78% Greek Orthodox,
18% Muslim, 4% other
Size: About half the size of Connecticut

LEBANON
Population: 3.7 million
Area: 3,950 sq. mi.
Government: Republic
Per Capita GDP: $5,200
Religion: 70% Muslim,
30% Christian
Size: About half the size of Connecticut

EGYPT
Population: 70.1 million
Area: 386,660 sq. mi.
Government: Republic
Per Capita GDP: $3,700
Religion: 94% Muslim,
6% Christian
Size: 3x New Mexico

SAUDI ARABIA
Population: 23.5 million
Area: 756,981 sq. mi.
Government: Monarchy
Per Capita GDP: $10,600
Religion: 99% Muslim, 1% othe
Size: 20 percent of the U.S.

ISRAEL
Population: 6 million
Area: 8,019 sq. mi.
Government: Parliamentary Democracy
Per Capita GDP: $19,000
Religion: 80% Jewish, 14% Muslim,
6% other
Size: slightly smaller than New Jersey

JORDAN
Population: 5.3 million
Area: 34,342 sq. mi.
Government: Constitutional Monarchy
Per Capita GDP: $4,300
Religion: 92% Muslim, 6% Christian,
2% other
Size: slightly smaller than Indiana

Map showing some of the major Middle Eastern countries

IRAQ
Population: 24 million
Area: 168,754 sq. mi.
Government: Republic
Per Capita GDP: $2,500
Religion: 97% Muslim, 3% Christian
Size: state of California

IRAN
Population: 66.6 million
Area: 636,293 sq. mi.
Government: Theocratic Republic
Per Capita GDP: $7,000
Religion: 99% Muslim, 1% other
Size: state of Alaska

KUWAIT
Population: 2.1 million
Area: 6,880 sq. mi.
Government: Nominal Constitutional Monarchy
Per Capita GDP: $15,100
Religion: 85% Muslim, 15% other
Size: slightly smaller than New Jersey

QATAR
Population: 793,341
Area: 4,416 sq. mi.
Government: Traditional Monarchy
Per Capita GDP: $21,200
Religion: 95% Muslim, 5% other
Size: state of Connecticut

BAHRAIN
Population: 656,397
Area: 262 sq. mi.
Government: Constitutional Heredity Monarchy
Per Capita GDP: $13,000
Religion: 99% Muslim, 1% other
Size: 3.5x Washington D.C.

UNITED ARAB EMIRATES
Population: 2.4 million
Area: 32,280 sq. mi.
Government: Federation with specified powers delegated to the UAE federal government and other powers reserved to member emirates
Per Capita GDP: $21,100
Religion: 96% Muslim, 4% other
Size: state of Maine

YEMEN
Population: 18.7 million
Area: 203,800 sq. mi.
Government: Republic
Per Capita GDP: $820
Religion: 99% Muslim, 1% other
Size: 2x state of Wyoming

OMAN
Population: 2.7 million
Area: 120,000 sq. mi.
Government: Monarchy
Per Capita GDP: $8,200
Religion: 90% Muslim, 10% other
Size: state of Kansas

EGYPT

Egypt is a North African country. Still, many consider it part of the Middle East. This country borders the Mediterranean Sea, the Red Sea, Libya, Sudan, the Gaza Strip, and Israel. It is the home of the world's longest river, which is the Nile. It is also home to the great pyramids.

The Western Desert covers much of Egypt, and only four percent of the land is fit for cultivation. Two inches of rain or less fall in this country each year. This is not enough to support the crops. Almost all food grown in Egypt is planted near the Nile. Water is channeled from the Nile to the crops.

By comparison, Egypt is just over three times the size of the state of New Mexico. Its land area covers 386,660 square miles.

Cairo is Egypt's capital city. About one fourth of the Egyptian population lives in and around the capital. It is one of the largest and fastest growing cities in Africa and the Middle East.

Egypt's population is about 70 million. Every 10 months about one million more people are added to the country's population count. Ninety-nine percent of Egyptians live along the Nile. Population problems are evident there and throughout the country. Egypt was once able to grow enough crops to support its people. Now the country depends on imported food from other

A map of Egypt

countries to feed its growing population. The country must deal with severe traffic problems and housing shortages. The housing problem is so serious that thousands of Egyptians live in the country's ancient cemeteries.

Ninety-nine percent of Egyptians are of Eastern Hamitic descent. Egypt's population includes Egyptians, Bedouins, and Berbers.

Ninety-four percent of the Egyptian population is Muslim. They are Sunni Muslims. Four to six percent of Egyptians are Christians. A very small number are Jewish. Egypt's Christians are called "Coptic Christians." These Christians, like other Christians, believe that Jesus was divine. The Copts are different because they don't believe Jesus was also fully human. These Christians have suffered at the hands of Muslim extremists.

Egypt's natural resources include petroleum, natural gas, iron ore, phosphates, manganese, and limestone. Gypsum, talc, asbestos, lead, and zinc are among its other natural resources. Egypt's primary income comes from textiles, food processing, tourism, chemicals, hydrocarbons, construction, cement, and metals.

Egypt has recorded its history for over 5,000 years. For most of these years, pharaohs or foreign rulers controlled Egypt. Modern Egyptian history is considered to have begun in the late eighteenth century. This is when Napoleon invaded the country. The French ruler introduced new ideas, the printing press, and an interest in modern science.

Britain granted Egypt some independence in 1922. The country's real independence didn't come, though, until 1952. Egyptian Colonel Gamal Nasser led a group of young soldiers in a bloodless overthrow of Egyptian King Farouk, a British loyalist.

Nasser became president of Egypt in 1954. He ruled until his death in 1970. Most Egyptians admired and mourned Nasser because he had secured Egypt's independence.

Anwar al-Sadat, Nasser's vice president, became Egypt's next leader. He sought closer ties to the U.S. and tried to introduce capitalism to the country. One of his most important accomplishments was making peace with Israel. For that, he won a Nobel Peace Prize. Islamic extremists assassinated him in 1981. The extremists thought Sadat was wrong for pursuing peace with Jews. Even the leaders of Arab countries were angered by the peace agreement. No Arab head of state attended Sadat's funeral.

Mohammed Hosni Mubarak became president of Egypt after Sadat's death. He focused on improving ties to other Arab nations. At the same time, he was careful not to weaken the country's relationship with the U.S.

Islamic extremist groups have tried to take over the Egyptian government on several occasions. One of the most notable and dangerous of those groups is called Gama'a al-Islamiya. The group's leader, Sheikh Omar Abdel Rahman, was also responsible for terrorism in the U.S. Rahman is now in a U.S. prison for life.

During the Gulf War, Egyptian President Mubarak had to decide whether to support the U.S. and its allies or Iraq. Mubarak decided to support the U.S. He sent Egyptian forces to help the U.S. in their attack on Iraq. The U.S. thanked Egypt for its support by forgiving Egypt's seven billion dollar debt.

Egypt's financial troubles have made the country dependent on help from other countries. The U.S. provides about half of this financial support. Those countries and organizations that support Egypt require the country to improve its economy.

Egypt's future depends upon its ability to stabilize its government. It must defend itself against extremist terrorist groups. The country must also improve its finances so that it can help its people improve their lives. None of these improvements will be easy, and none of them will happen overnight.

The sultan's mosque and Cairo skyline in Egypt.

IRAN

Afghanistan, Azerbaijan, Iraq, Pakistan, Turkey, and Turkmenistan border Iran. The Gulf of Oman, the Persian Gulf, and the Caspian Sea surround Iran. The country sits on a plateau that is 4,000 feet high. Mountain ranges almost completely surround this plateau. Only one inch of rain or less falls in Iran's central plateau annually. About 50 inches fall in the western mountains.

Deserts also cover much of Iran. Iran's deserts and mountains have acted as natural barriers, keeping ethnic groups separate from each other. Often these ethnic groups are more loyal to their group than they are to their country.

Iran's land area covers 636,293 square miles. The country is close in size to Alaska, the largest state in the U.S.

The population of Iran is 66 million. Its capital, Tehran, is among the country's most populated cities. Other highly populated cities are Bushehr, Kermanshah, and Tabriz.

Iran's population is made up of people with Persian, Azeri, Gilaki and Mazandarani, Kurd, Arab, Lur, Baloch, and Turkmen roots. About 51 percent of the population is Persian. Though some Persians live in Iran's central mountain valleys, most live in cities. They form the majority of the country's upper class. Since 1502, all Iranian rulers have been Persian.

A map of Iran

Most of Iran's population is Muslim. Eighty-nine percent are Shiite Muslims. Ten percent are Sunni Muslims. The remaining one percent are Zoroastrian, Jewish, Christian, or Baha'i. Iran is one of the few Middle Eastern countries with a larger number of Shiites than Sunnis. Shiite leaders have played a central role in governing the country.

Iran has access to trade routes because three major bodies of water surround it. This access allows Iran to ship its natural resources. The country's most important natural resource, like many Middle Eastern countries, is oil. Other resources include coal, chromium, copper, iron ore, lead, manganese, zinc, and sulfur.

Products from its industries also boost Iran's economy. The country produces textiles, cement, and other construction materials. It also processes food and makes metals and weapons.

Iran has been civilized for more than 25 centuries. It has been under Persian, Greek, and Roman rule. Modern Iranian history began in 1905. A parliament was created and a constitution was introduced in 1906.

Within the last century, Mohammad Reza ruled Iran for 37 years. He was also called the Shah of Iran. Reza had close ties with the U.S. government. The U.S. depended on Reza for oil and to keep communism out of the country. Reza depended on the U.S. for military equipment. During his rule, Reza promoted women's right to vote and improved health care and education. Many Muslims were angered by Reza's actions and his tight relationship with the West. They felt that Western values were threatening to Islamic ones.

In 1979, many Iranians revolted against Reza. The Ayatollah Ruholla Khomeini, a religious leader, planned this revolt, which ended Reza's rule. Reza left Iran when he realized

he could not keep power. In April 1979, the Islamic Republic of Iran was declared.

From 1979 until 1989, Khomeini was Iran's political and religious leader. The constitution, which was drafted in 1979, gave the religious leader final authority in government matters. Khomeini even had power over the country's president.

Iran has not had peaceful relationships with its Arab neighbors. The country's longest active conflict was with Iraq. In the late 1980s, Khomeini realized the threat of losing land to Iraq. Hundreds of thousands of Iranians had died, and Iran was bankrupt. Khomeini agreed to a UN peace plan. Eventually the fighting between Iran and Iraq stopped.

When Khomeini died in 1989, the country mourned. Ali Khamenei took over as Iran's supreme leader. Some loosening of government controls over cultural practices came with the change in religious leadership.

In 1997, Mohammad Khatemi won Iran's presidential elections. He was not the religious leaders' choice for president. The religious leaders thought he was too liberal. The majority of Iranian citizens, though, were ready for the change Khatemi represented. Young people and women, especially, supported him.

Iran's reputation has improved in the West since Khatemi's election. Still, Khatemi remains committed to building up nuclear weapons. He hopes these weapons will protect it from the U.S. and other Western nations. Meanwhile, Khatemi drives for economic and policy changes within his country. He also works to improve Iran's reputation within the Arab community and with Western nations, too.

Iranian Baseej militia women march

IRAQ

Iraq is located on the northern end of the Persian Gulf. It borders Iran, Turkey, Syria, Jordan, Saudi Arabia, and Kuwait. Iraq is almost entirely landlocked and has only 30 miles of coastline. This coastline, which connects to the Persian Gulf, is home to two major ports. Iraq's landscape is made up of vast plains, deserts, and marshlands. Mountains span the Iraqi borders along Iran and Turkey.

Iraq's territory covers 168,754 square miles. It is roughly the size of California. The nation's southern border is largely covered by the Syrian Desert. Its northern regions include Iraqi highlands around the cities of Mosul and Kirkuk.

The capital of Iraq is Baghdad. Almost five million people live in this city located near the Tigris River. This city is also home to some of the Iraqi government's largest palaces. The living quarters of many high-ranking officials in the Iraqi army are also in Baghdad.

Seventy-five to eighty percent of Iraq's population is Arab. Fifteen to twenty percent of the population is Kurdish. About five percent is made up of Turkomen, Assyrian, and people from other backgrounds.

Map of Iraq

Ninety-seven percent of Iraqi people are Muslim. The remaining three percent of Iraqis practice Christianity or other religions. While most Muslims are Sunnis, over half of Iraq's Muslims are Shiite. The Shiite religion actually began in Iraq. The Shiites' holiest cities, Najaf and Karbala, are located in Iraq. The Kurds, Iraq's largest minority group, are typically Sunni Muslims.

Iraq's chief industry is oil. The country is one of the world's leaders in total oil earnings. In addition to oil, the country also has resources in natural gas and limestone. Much of Iraq's land also has great agricultural potential. This potential has not been fully realized.

Iraq received its independence from the British-led League of Nations on October 3, 1932. The British had originally conquered Iraq in 1920 after World War I. Even after Iraq was granted independence, the British influence, within the nation's borders, remained. Iraq finally split from British influence in 1959 when the Iraqi government withdrew from the Baghdad Pact. The goal of the Baghdad Pact was to develop a unified opposition against Soviet presence in the region. The United States and Britain were part of this pact.

Iraq then went through a series of coups. The Socialist Resurrection Party, known as Ba'th, took power in 1968. Saddam Hussein, a member of this party, rose to power in Iraq in 1979.

Iraq's government is called a republic. The reality is that, under Saddam, it functions as more of a dictatorship. Saddam Hussein and the Ba'th party are known for human rights

Iraqi girls celebrating the birthday of Saddam Hussein

violations. Many of these violations have involved the Kurdish population that lives in the nation's northern mountains. Still today, the Kurdish opposition remains a real threat in Iraq. Different factions would like to remove Saddam as ruler of Iraq.

Iraq's biggest challenge involves its ongoing conflict with the U.S. This conflict escalated in 1991 when the U.S. and its allies defeated Iraq in what became known as the Persian Gulf War.

Today, the United States is in conflict with Iraq once again. The U.S. government believes that the Iraqi government owns weapons of mass destruction. The UN weapons inspectors went into Iraq in late 2002 to search for weapons of mass destruction.

U.S. President George W. Bush was not convinced Iraq had gotten rid of its weapons of mass destruction. Bush wanted the UN to stand behind a U.S. led attack against the Iraqi government. Some UN countries supported Bush. Others wanted to allow Iraq more time to disarm.

Without the full support of the UN, on March 17, 2003, Bush gave Saddam Hussein 48 hours to leave Iraq. On March 19, the U.S. and its allies began the war against Saddam's regime.

ISRAEL

Israel was created on the territory previously known as Palestine. Israel's neighbors are Egypt, Jordan, Lebanon, Syria, the Gaza Strip, and the West Bank. The Mediterranean Sea borders Israel's west side.

Israel is made up of a productive hilly region, a low coastal plain, where most of the population lives, and the Negev desert region. The Jordan Rift Valley is on Israel's east side near its border with Jordan.

Israel covers 8,019 square miles. This means it is slightly smaller than the state of New Jersey.

In 1950, Israel claimed Jerusalem as its capital. The Palestinians also claim Jerusalem as theirs. The U.S. and most other countries maintain their Israeli embassies in Tel Aviv.

The population of Israel is just over 6 million. About 57 percent of Israelis were born in Israel, and about 24 percent are from Europe and the western hemisphere. Nineteen percent are from Africa or Asia.

Almost 80 percent of Israelis are Jewish. The remainder of the population is Arab. Most of these Arabs are Muslim. A small number are Christians or followers of other religions. Although

A map of Israel

Israel says its Arab citizens are "full citizens of state," they are treated differently than their Jewish counterparts. The Arabs don't receive the same quality of education, housing, or social services that the Jews do. The Arabs also cannot work in Israeli jobs that are security related.

Israel has far fewer natural resources than other Middle Eastern countries. It has small amounts of timber, potash, copper ore, and natural gas. Phosphate rock, magnesium bromide, clay, and sand are also found here. There are not enough natural resources to support Israel's economy. This means the country must make money in other ways.

The country's other major sources of income are the sale of computer software and medical equipment. The country also sells telecommunications equipment. Other Israeli products include wood and paper, tobacco, beverages, caustic soda, and cement. Israel's major industries are diamond-cutting and weapons production.

Israel has been in conflict since it was declared independent in 1948. Israel is a Jewish nation. Palestine, like most other Arab countries, is Muslim. The core of the problem is the land dispute between Israel and Palestine. Both Muslims and Jews consider parts of this land holy. Each group has gained and lost land to each other. Other Middle Eastern countries have also been involved in this land dispute. Most Arab nations support Palestine.

Israel has received support in the form of weapons and money from Western countries. Its biggest ally has been the U.S. The United States' support of Israel has caused tension between the U.S. and many Arab nations.

Dome of the Rock behind Jewish cemetery, Jerusalem

Israel's government consists of a legislature, prime minister, cabinet, and president. The president is considered the head of state. Israel's prime minister holds more power than its president and leads the government and the cabinet. Israel's current prime minister, Ariel Sharon, was elected to office in 2001.

While Sharon talks of peace between Israel and Arab countries, he has said publicly that his priority is the security of his country. Sharon's challenges include the continued control of Muslim extremist groups. These extremists are angry about the Jewish control of land they consider theirs. They continue to attack Israelis through suicide bombings. As a nation surrounded by enemies, the Israel government focuses primarily on the country's survival.

SAUDI ARABIA

Saudi Arabia is one of the largest nations in the Middle East. The country borders Jordan, Iraq, Kuwait, Qatar, the United Arab Emirates, Oman, and Yemen. The Red Sea and the Persian Gulf also border Saudi Arabia.

Saudi Arabia is a dry desert country. The country has no natural rivers or lasting bodies of water. The majority of the land receives between two to four inches of rain a year. In the Rub al-Khali desert, there have been times when no rain fell for 10 years. The Asir region is one of the few areas in Saudi Arabia that receives rain. An average of 20 inches a year falls there.

Roughly one-fifth the size of the U.S., Saudi Arabia spans 756,981 square miles. The capital of Saudi Arabia is the city Riyadh. The city has more than 1.3 million people living in it. Riyadh is located in the center of the country and is closer to the Persian Gulf than the Red Sea.

About 23 million people live in Saudi Arabia. This country has a very homogenous society. Ninety percent of the nation's people are of Arab descent. The remaining 10 percent of the population is Afro-Asian.

A map of Saudi Arabia

Nearly every person in Saudi Arabia follows the religion of Islam. Most of these followers are Sunni Muslims. The Shiite Muslims of Saudi Arabia live in the oil-rich eastern province.

Saudi Arabia's main economic resource is oil. The nation has the largest oil reserves in the world and it is the second largest oil exporter. Oil makes up 75 percent of the nation's revenue. Only 25 percent of the country's revenue comes from privately held businesses. While Saudi Arabia is strong in oil production, it is sorely lacking fresh water and agriculture products. Saudi Arabia is also lacking in workers. Saudi citizens make up only 10 percent of the nation's workforce. Many management jobs go to people from Western nations. People from other Middle Eastern nations typically fill labor positions.

The region that makes up Saudi Arabia has a long history of foreign rule. The modern country as we know it didn't take its current shape until 1932. On September 24 of that year, an Arab leader named Abd al-Aziz unified the groups Hijaz and Najd and their dependents and formed the Kingdom of Saudi Arabia. The Kingdom has been ruled by family members from the house of Saud ever since.

Saudi Arabia is an absolute monarchy. It has both a king and a crown prince. The crown prince is the heir apparent to the throne. This means that the prince assumes the crown should anything happen to the king. The Koran, the Muslims' holy book, as well as Shari'a, Islamic Law, serve as the nation's constitution. A panel of crown princes makes major national decisions. There are about 4,000 crown princes currently in Saudi Arabia. Most do not play a major role in the government.

Masjid an-Nabawi Minarets in Medina, Saudi Arabia at twilight

Any government legislation must follow what is written in the Koran. The king serves as the final appeal for any long standing conflicts. Alcohol is not allowed in Saudi Arabia and men and women are segregated. This means that they are kept separate. Lawbreakers must face Shari'a punishment, which is often brutal. Political parties and unions are not allowed in Saudi Arabia.

The Saudi nation faces many challenges. Because the country's economy is so dependent on oil, the wealth of the country changes with the price of oil. Efforts are being made to improve the country's other domestic economic options. The country does not want to be dependent on just one revenue resource. Saudi Arabia must also continuously find ways to replenish its water supply.

As the nation tries to expand business outside the Middle East, it risks being attacked. Saudi Arabian Islamic extremists typically wage these attacks. The extremists don't like the Saudi government's ties to Western nations like the U.S. Osama bin Laden was a Saudi citizen until the government made him leave. He had expressed hostility towards what he calls the "Westernized Saudi regime." After bin Laden left Saudi Arabia, he became known as the terrorist responsible for planning the September 11, 2001, attacks against the U.S. The threat of Islamic extremists continues.

SYRIA

Syria is bordered by the Middle Eastern countries of Iraq, Jordan, Israel, Lebanon, and Turkey. The country is made up of an inland plateau and a coastal zone. Within the coastal zone, two mountain ranges enclose fertile lowlands. The Hamad desert region is located in the southeastern part of the country.

The Euphrates River enters Syria from the north. It flows southwest across the country and exits into neighboring Iraq. This river supplies the country with 80 percent of the water it needs. The Mediterranean Sea borders Syria's west side. Access to the sea provides Syria with a valuable source of income. The country profits from two pipelines that transport petroleum from neighboring Gulf countries to the Mediterranean.

Syria has a total land area of 71,498 square miles. It is slightly larger than the state of North Dakota. Within Syria's total land area, is 500 square miles of the Golan Heights. Israel took the Golan Heights from Syria in 1967. The Golan Heights became Israel's after the small, Jewish country defeated Syria and several other Arab countries in the Six-Day War. The Golan Heights remains part of Israeli territory, and Syria and Israel remain at odds.

A map of Syria

Syria's capital city of Damascus is located in the southwestern part of the country. Historians believe that Damascus was settled as early as 2500 B.C. This makes it one of the world's oldest, continuously inhabited cities.

The population of Syria is about 17 million. Arabs make up the country's main ethnic group at 90 percent of the population. The other 10 percent is made up of Kurds, Armenians, and people of other nationalities.

Seventy-four percent of the Syrian population is Sunni Muslim. Sixteen percent is Alawite, Druze, or from other Muslim groups. Christians make up 10 percent of the population. A few Jewish communities make up less than one percent of the total population.

Syria has fewer oil and gas deposits than many of its neighbors. The country supports itself by producing and exporting what petroleum it does have. Syria's other exports include textiles, fruits, vegetables, and raw cotton. The country also produces table salt from its salt lakes.

For thousands of years, foreign rulers controlled Syria. This country only gained its independence from France in 1946. Between 1946 and 1970, Syria experienced great political instability. During this time of instability, the country became known as the Arab state most likely to experience a military takeover.

Hafiz al-Asad was successful in taking control of Syria in the early 1970s. As an Alawite, Asad was part of the religious minority. It was surprising for him to be able to control a country where more than 74 percent of the population was Sunni Muslim.

He established a republic that had executive, legislative, and judicial branches. His presidency brought stability to the country until his death in 2000.

Asad's government was stable, but far from perfect. Power was not spread among the Syrian people, and Asad did not tolerate those who opposed him. His government was also known for its human rights violations against the Palestinians and Lebanese.

Syria became known, too, for harboring terrorists. The United States' government had labeled Syria a "state that sponsored terrorism."

Since 1976, Syria has had troops stationed in Lebanon. Syria quickly established itself as being politically and militarily supreme. By 1990, Lebanon no longer resisted Syria's control.

Syria played a role in the 1991 Persian Gulf War. Iraq had surprised the U.S. government when it attacked Kuwait. Syrian President Hafiz al Asad sided with the U.S. against Iraq. This helped the U.S. defend its ally and its interests in Kuwait. In exchange, Syria received $1.5 billion from Western nations.

The United States and Soviet Union issued a joint invitation to Israel and its Arab neighbors. The U.S. and Soviet Union wanted peace in the Middle East. Syria's President Asad went to the peace talks in Madrid, Spain, in 1991. He discussed Syria's idea to return the Golan Heights to Palestine. No agreement was reached.

The city of Damascus at night

Syria continues to face major issues. Its growing population means an increased need for water. The country will need to work out water sharing agreements with its neighbors, Turkey and Iraq. The flow of the Euphrates is at issue. Syria has also made efforts to change its reputation as a nation that sponsors terrorism. It has stopped Palestinian groups in Damascus from carrying out violence. It has also forced a terrorist leader from the country.

Bashar al-Asad, Hafiz's son, has ruled Syria since his father's death. He will face challenges of his own as a relatively new leader of a complex nation.

The countries of the Middle East, though different from each other, share much in common. The majority of Middle Easterners are Arab. These countries have shared history, as many were part of the Ottoman and/or Roman empires. Most also share a common religion, which is Islam. Israel, which is mainly Jewish, is the only exception. Many Middle Eastern countries are also rich in oil. This fact continues to draw the attention of other nations around the world.

WEB SITES
WWW.ABDOPUB.COM

Would you like to learn more about Countries of the Middle East? Please visit www.abdopub.com to find up-to-date Web site links about Countries of the Middle East and the World in Conflict. These links are routinely monitored and updated to provide the most current information available.

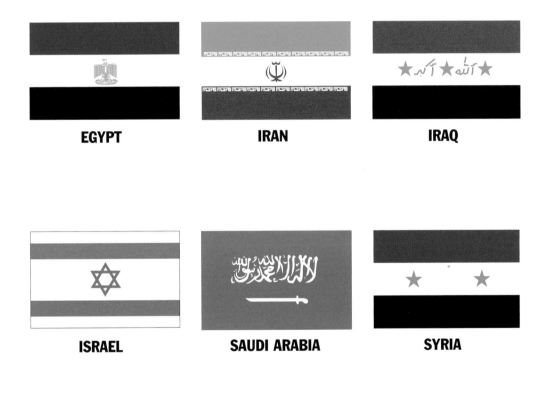

EGYPT **IRAN** **IRAQ**

ISRAEL **SAUDI ARABIA** **SYRIA**

Flags of six major Middle Eastern countries

TIMELINE

1922	On February 28, Egypt gains its independence from the United Kingdom.
1932	Saudi Arabia gains independence on September 23.
	Iraq gains independence on October 3.
1946	Syria gains independence on April 17.
1948	Israel declares itself an independent nation. Egypt, Iraq, Lebanon, and Syria attack Israel.
1967	Israel battles Egypt, Iraq, Jordan, and Syria in the Six Day War. Israel gains control of the Golan Heights, the West Bank, the Gaza Strip, and the Sinai Peninsula. Israel sets up Jewish settlements in these territories.
1973	Yom Kippur War. Egypt and Syria attack Israel.

1979	Iranian Revolution results in overthrow of U.S.-friendly government. Islamic fundamentalist government is established in Iran. Islamic Republic of Iran is proclaimed.
1980	Iraq launches war against Iran.
1988	Iran and Iraq accept UN call for a cease-fire.
1990	Iraq attacks Kuwait in an attempt to take over its oil supply.
1991	Persian Gulf War. The U.S. leads an attack against Iraq.
Early 1990s	UN weapons inspectors search for weapons of mass destruction in Iraq.
2001	Middle Eastern terrorists seize commercial airliners and drive them into American targets on September 11.
2002- 2003	UN weapons inspectors search for weapons of mass destruction in Iraq.
2003	U.S. and coalition forces attack Iraq on March 19.

FAST FACTS

Country:	**Egypt**
Capital:	Cairo
Climate:	desert; hot, dry summers with moderate winters
Life expectancy at birth:	64.05 years
Government type:	Republic
Independence:	February 28, 1922 (from United Kingdom)
External debt:	$29 billion (2001 estimate)

Country:	**Iran**
Capital:	Tehran
Climate:	mostly arid or semiarid, subtropical along Caspian coast
Life expectancy at birth:	70.25 years for total population
Government type:	Theocratic republic
Independence:	April 1, 1979 (Islamic Republic of Iran proclaimed)
External debt:	$7.3 billion (2001 estimate)

Country:	**Iraq**
Capital:	Baghdad
Climate:	Mostly desert; mild to cool winters with dry, hot, cloudless summers; northern mountainous regions along Iranian and Turkish borders experience cold winters with occasionally heavy snows that melt in early spring, sometimes causing extensive flooding in central and southern Iraq
Life expectancy at birth:	67.38 years for total population
Government type:	Republic
Independence:	October 3, 1932 (from League of Nations mandate under British administration)
External debt:	$62.2 billion (2001 estimate)

Country:	Israel
Capital:	Jerusalem (the U.S. still maintains its embassy in Tel Aviv)
Climate:	temperate; hot and dry in southern and eastern desert areas
Life expectancy at birth:	78.86 years for total population
Government type:	Parliamentary democracy
Independence:	May 14, 1948 (from League of Nations mandate under British administration)
External debt:	$42.8 billion (2001 estimate)

Country:	Saudi Arabia
Capital:	Riyadh
Climate:	harsh, dry desert with great temperature extremes
Life expectancy at birth:	68.4 years
Government type:	Monarchy
Independence:	September 23, 1932 (Unification of the Kingdom)
External debt:	$23.8 billion (by 2001 estimate)

Country:	Syria
Capital:	Damascus
Climate:	Mostly desert; hot, dry, sunny summers (June to August) and mild, rainy winters (December to February) along coast; cold weather with snow or sleet periodically in Damascus
Life expectancy at birth:	69.08 years for total population
Government type:	Republic under military regime since March 1963
Independence:	April 17, 1946 (from League of Nations under French administration)
External debt:	$22 billion (2001 estimate)

(All Fast Facts taken from the CIA World Factbook 2002)

GLOSSARY

Afghanistan: a Middle Eastern country.

Alawite: an offshoot of Shiite Islam.

Algeria: a Middle Eastern country.

ally: a friend; a person or group of people against the same enemy.

Arabs: people whose ancestors were from Arabia.

Armenians: those who live in Armenia, a country in southwestern Asia.

Asad, Hafiz al: president of Syria from 1971 until 2000.

asbestos: mineral that builders use to fireproof buildings.

Assyrian: person whose ancestors were from Assyria, an ancient empire of western Asia.

Azerbaijan: a Middle Eastern country.

Azeri: Shiite Muslim person from Azerbaijan.

Baha'i: a religion founded in 1863 in Persia that focuses on the spiritual unity of all humans.

Bahrain: a Middle Eastern country.

Baloch: an Iranian ethnic group.

Bedouins: Arabic-speaking people of the Middle East deserts.

Berbers: people whose ancestors were pre-Arab dwellers of North Africa.

bin Laden, Osama: a radical Islamic fundamentalist from Saudi Arabia who is thought to have masterminded the September 11, 2001 terrorist attacks against the U.S.

Bushehr: a city in Iran.

Caspian Sea: world's largest inland body of water; the Caspian Sea is to the west of Central Asia.

caustic soda: ashes used in making glass.

chemical weapons: highly dangerous man-made substances that are dispersed in liquid or gas forms to harm large portions of the enemy's population.

Christian: major world religion that is based on the life and teachings of Jesus Christ.

chromium: metallic element used to produce stainless steel.

coup: the removal of a person in power.

Damascus: capital city of Syria.

Druze: small Middle East religious sect.

extremist: one who resorts to measures beyond what is normal.

Gama'a al-Islamiya: a radical Islamic terrorist group in Egypt.

Gaza Strip: narrow strip of land along the Mediterranean Sea near the city of Gaza.

Gilaki: an Iranian ethnic group.

Golan Heights: hilly area that overlooks the Jordan River Valley. Under Israeli military control since 1981.

Gulf of Oman: northwest portion of the Arabian Sea.

gypsum: mineral used to make plastic products and fertilizer.

Hamitic: a group of North African languages.

head of state: the leader of a country.

Homogenous: alike in nature; consistent, sameness.

Hussein, Saddam: president of Iraq since 1979.

hydrocarbons: an organic compound that contains only carbon and hydrogen.

Iran: a Middle Eastern country.

Iraq: a Middle Eastern country.

Islam: a monotheistic religion started by the Prophet Muhammad.

Israel: a Middle Eastern country.

Jew (Jewish): any person whose religion is Judaism.

Jordan: a Middle Eastern country.

Judaism: monotheistic religion of the Jews.

Kazakhstan: a Middle Eastern country.

Kermanshah: a city in western Iran.

Khatemi, Mohammad: president of Iran since 1997.

Khomeini, Ayatollah Ruhollah: Iranian Shiite cleric who led the country's revolution. He was Iran's leader from 1979 - 1989.

Kurds: those who were born or live in the mountainous area of West Asia.

Kuwait: a Middle Eastern country.

Kyrgyzstan: a republic in west central Asia.

landlocked: entirely or almost entirely surrounded by land.

lead: a soft metallic element.

League of Nations: an organization established in 1920 to promote world peace. Existed before the United Nations was formed.

Lebanon: a Middle Eastern country.

Libya: a Middle Eastern country.

limestone: rock used as building stone.

loyalist: one who remains loyal to the government in power.

magnesium: a metallic element.

manganese: a metallic element.

Mazandarani: an Iranian ethnic group.

Mediterranean Sea: the largest inland sea located between Europe, Africa, and Asia.

Morocco: a Middle Eastern country.

Muslim: a believer of Islam; the Islamic religion is based on the teaching of Muhammad.

Oman: a sultan-led country of the Southeast Arabian Peninsula.

Operation Desert Storm: the 1991 U.S.-led attack against Iraq.

Ottoman Empire: sultan-ruled land of southwest Asia, northeast Africa, and southeast Europe.

Pakistan: a Middle Eastern country.

Palestinian: a person who lives in Palestine; a region in the Middle East.

Persian Gulf War: a war in which the U.S. and its allies freed Kuwait from Iraq.

petroleum: a mixture of gas, liquid, and solid materials found beneath the earth's surface. Can be turned into gas, gasoline, fuel, and asphalt.

phosphate: a salt.

potash: a compound that contains potassium.

Qatar: a Middle Eastern country.

Rahman, Sheikh Omar Abdel: leader of Egyptian radical Islamic group.

Riyadh: the capital of Saudi Arabia.

Saudi Arabia: a Middle Eastern country.

Shiite Muslim: these Muslims believe Mohammad chose his own successor.

Sudan: a Middle Eastern country.

Sunni Muslim: the original Sunni Muslims believed that they should vote for Mohammad's successor.

Syria: a Middle Eastern country.

Tabriz: a city in northwest Iran.

Tajikistan: a Middle Eastern country.

talc: a mineral.

Tehran: the capital of Iran.

telecommunication: electronic systems used in transmitting information. Examples are the telegraph, cable, telephone, TV, and radio.

terrorism: the illegal use of violence by a person or group of people with the intention of intimidating a society or government.

textile: a cloth, typically one that is woven or knitted.

tourism: the practice of traveling for pleasure.

Tunisia: a Middle Eastern country.

Turkmenistan: a Middle Eastern country.

Turkey: a Middle Eastern country.

Turkoman: one who was born or lives in Turkmenistan.

United Arab Emirates: a Middle Eastern country.

United Nations: an international organization started in 1945 to promote peace, security, and economic development across the world.

United States: a country in North America.

Uzbekistan: a Middle Eastern country.

weapon of mass destruction: an instrument of attack that causes injury and/or death to large numbers of people at one time.

West Bank: Middle East territory between Israel and Jordan.

Western countries: nations in the western hemisphere that typically have high Christian populations.

Yemen: a Middle Eastern country.

zinc: a metallic element.

Zoroastrian: a religion that teaches the worship of Ahura Mazda. Addresses the universal struggle between the forces of light and darkness.

INDEX

A
Afghanistan 4, 13
Al-Asad, Bashar 38
Al-Asad, Hafiz 35
Al-Sadat, Anwar 11
Alawite 35
Algeria 4
Arabian desert 8, 18
Armenians 35
Assyrian 18
Azerbaijan 13
Azeri 13
B
Baghdad 6, 18, 19, 20, 42
Baha'i 15
Bahrain 4
Baloch 13
Bedouins 10
Berbers 10
Bin Laden, Osama 5, 31
Britain 10, 20
Bushehr 13
C
Christians 10, 15, 23, 35
Coptic Christian 10
D
Damascus 34, 35, 37, 38, 43
Druze 35
F
Farouk, King 10
G
Gama'a al-Islamiya 11
Gaza Strip 8, 23, 24
Gilaki 13
Golan Heights 33, 36, 40
Gulf of Oman 13, 14
Gulf War 11, 22, 36, 41
H
Hussein, Saddam 20, 21, 22

I
Iran 4, 7, 13, 14, 15, 16, 18,
    39, 41, 42
Iraq 4, 7, 11, 13, 16, 18, 19,
    20, 22, 28, 33, 36, 38, 39,
    40, 41, 42
Israel 4, 5, 6, 8, 11, 23, 24,
    25, 27, 33, 36, 38, 39,
    40, 43
J
Jerusalem 6, 23, 24, 26, 43
Jordan 4, 6, 18, 23, 28, 33, 40
K
Kazakhstan 4
Kermanshah 13
Khatemi, Mohammad 16
Khomeini, Ayatollah
    Ruholla 15
Kurds 20, 35
Kuwait 4, 7, 18, 28, 36, 41
Kyrgyzstan 4
L
Lebanon 4, 6, 23, 33, 36, 40
Libya 4, 8
M
Mazandarani 13
Morocco 4
Mubarak, Hosni 11
N
Napoleon 10
Nasser, Gamal 10, 11
O
Oman 4, 7, 28
Ottoman Empire 38
P
Pakistan 4, 13
Palestinian 5, 38
Persian Gulf War 22, 36, 41
Q
Qatar 4

R
Rahman, Sheikh Omar
    Abdel 11
Reza, Mohammad 15
Riyadh 7, 28, 43
S
Saudi Arabia 4, 6, 18, 28, 29,
    30, 31, 39, 40, 43
Sharon, Ariel 27
Shiite Muslim 15, 20, 30
Six-Day War 33
Sudan 4, 8
Sunni Muslim 10, 15, 20,
    30, 35
Syria 6, 18, 23, 33, 34, 35,
    36, 38, 39, 40, 43
T
Tabriz 13
Tajikistan 4
Tehran 7, 13, 42
Terrorist 5, 12, 31, 38,
Tunisia 4
Turkmenistan 4, 13
Turkey 4, 6, 13, 18, 33, 38
Turkomen 18
U
United Arab Emirates 4, 7,
28
United Nations (UN) 11, 16,
    21, 41
United States (U.S.) 4, 5, 11,
    13, 15, 16, 20, 22, 23, 25,
    31, 36, 41, 43
Uzbekistan 4
W
West Bank 23, 24, 40
Y
Yemen 4, 7, 28
Z
Zoroastrian 15